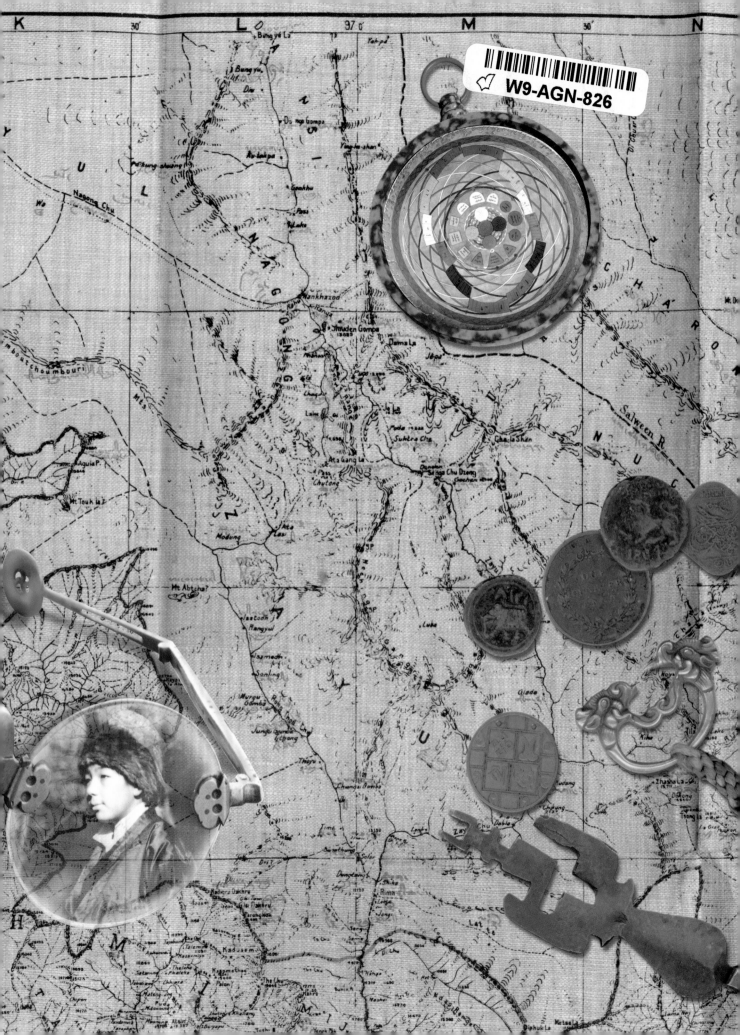

A Dog's Tooth

This book belongs to:

_____

_____

and friends.

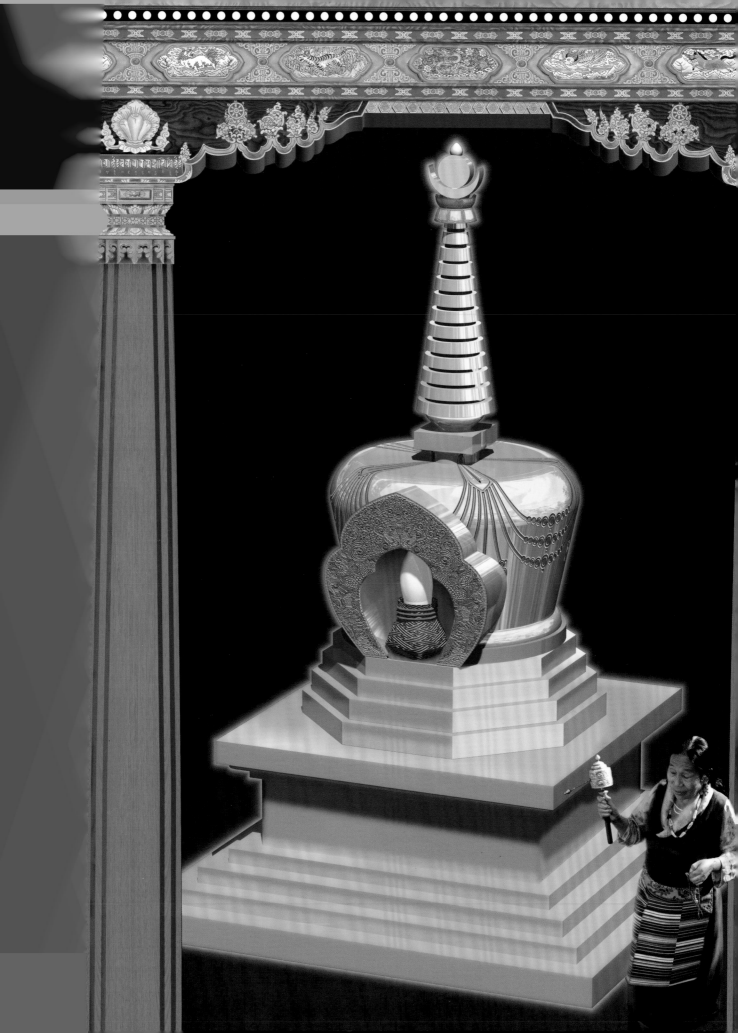

A Dog's Tooth

by W.W. Rowe

illustrated by Chris Banigan

SNOW LION PUBLICATIONS

Snow Lion Publications

P.O. Box 6483, Ithaca, New York 14851
tel: 607-273-8519

ISBN 1-55939-087-5

Library of Congress Cataloging-in-Publication Data

Rowe, William Woodin.
     A dog's tooth / by W.W. Rowe; illustrated by Chris Banigan.
          p.   cm.
          Summary: A retelling of the Tibetan tale of deception and faith in which a young
man who fails to obtain a sacred relic for his dying mother gives her a dog's tooth instead.
     ISBN 1-55939-087-5
     [1. Folklore, Tibet.]   I. Banigan,   Christopher, ill.
     II. Title.
     PZ8. 1. R837Do   1998
     398. 2' 0951'5--dc21   97-40186
     [E]   CIP
                                                                                       AC

Printed in Singapore.

for Eleanor

বাউ'ব

Many years ago in Tibet, there lived a boy named Ösel. And though you might not guess it to look at him, the lad was sneaky smart.

Ösel could fool almost anyone. The rascal spent much of his time plotting and scheming. And he seemed so innocent! His playmates never suspected what was happening–until too late.

One summer day, Ösel went to see another boy. "Come on," he whispered. "Something new . . . a secret thing to share with you."

He led his friend down to a little stream. Then, glancing about suspiciously, he pulled out a smooth, round stone. It was grey with little dark specks. Ösel held it carefully in his palm, like an egg that might break.

"I'll bet you'd really like to own this good luck charm," he said, smiling proudly. "It's called a talisman. It has amazing powers."

The friend's eyes grew wide. "Shouldn't it have writing on it?"

"Writing?" said Ösel.

"Yes. Mystic symbols or something."

Ösel looked shocked. "Are you kidding? Mystic symbols might spoil the magic. This talisman belonged to a very wise man. It made him rich his whole life long. It kept him safe and wise and strong."

Ösel praised the stone so cleverly, his friend just itched to have it. The friend began to beg: "I'll give you my new slingshot, my next piece of pie. . . I'll even give you this silver coin. It's very rare! It really is, Ösel, I swear. Just let me have the talisman!" He had a wild gleam in his eyes.

"Oh, well." Ösel shrugged. "Why not? I'm feeling generous today."

His friend let out a yelp of glee. "Oh, thank you, Ösel! Thank you!"

No sooner had he left, than Ösel smiled slyly and went off to see another friend. "Let's go to the pine grove," he said, winking confidentially. "I've got something secret to show you."

Deep among the fir trees, Ösel revealed a light-brown stone. "This," he whispered, "is a talisman."

"A what?" The friend squinted. "Looks like a plain old rock to me."

"Oh, come on!" Ösel snorted scornfully. "Don't you know anything? A talisman is a magical charm. It has amazing powers. This one belonged to a very wise man. It made him rich his whole life long. It kept him safe and wise and strong."

"For shame!" Ösel's mother told him. "It's wrong to cheat. You will destroy the trust and faith of all your friends. Deceitful deeds have bitter ends."

But Ösel's father was proud of him. "I understand," he said. "Our son has a great talent for making deals. Just like me. To bargain is not a shame; stealing is shameful." He paused, smiling. "Our Ösel is going to be very rich. He's smart. He's shrewd. He can't just play. He'll trick the gods themselves one day."

Ösel's father traded precious metals. He often journeyed to distant lands. His next trip was south to India, with gold, and he had to cross a high mountain pass.

Part way up, the path curved between narrow rock walls. All of a sudden, wild bandits with swords and daggers dropped down before him. More bandits closed in from behind. Alas, he and his load of gold were never seen again.

When he failed to return, Ösel's mother had to raise the boy herself. At first, it was painfully hard. They were very poor. They suffered greatly. But then Ösel became a successful trader– and the money flowed in like melted snow down a mountain stream.

Ösel's mother wore the finest clothes and always, in her hair, turquoise, coral, and silver ornaments. Ösel drank the best barley beer. He ate fresh fruits. He wore billowy silk shirts and rode a spirited, brown horse. His mother smiled. She loved to see him all decked out so handsomely.

Five years passed. One day, Ösel's mother declared: "My son, it's true. We are most fortunate, but dangers and disaster could be lurking nearby."

"Ama-la!" Ösel exclaimed. "We have known much suffering. Let us enjoy our happiness."

"So we do, my son. And I am grateful. But this will not last forever. You really should devote more time to prayer– or you will wish you had, some day."

"Don't worry, Ama-la," Ösel replied. "For me, dangers are like a misty fog that vanishes before the rising sun. I'm smart as a young tiger, rich and strong, so what could possibly go wrong?"

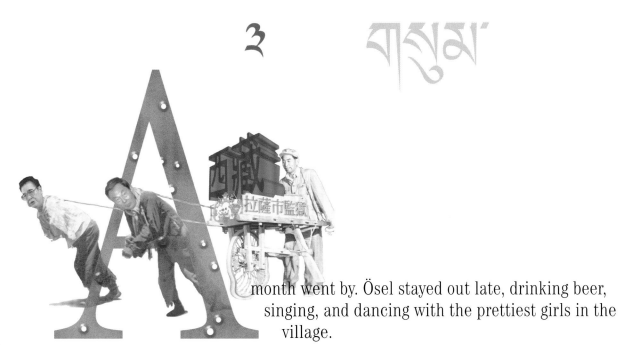

3　　གསུམ

A month went by. Ösel stayed out late, drinking beer, singing, and dancing with the prettiest girls in the village.

One morning, his mother awoke with a sore neck. The pain slowly spread.

"Ah-ru!" she moaned. "It hurts so much! Please fetch the doctor, Ösel."

"Yes, Ama-la. I'll ride faster than the wind!"

He soon returned, pushing an old, bald man into the house.

The doctor carefully examined Ösel's mother, sighed, and said: "I fear there's not much I can do. But take this medicine."

When he had gone, she turned to Ösel. "My son, please listen. I'll take this medicine, but . . . What I need is a sacred relic from Bodh Gaya, where the Buddha went to reach his great enlightenment. It will help me pray for all beings. A relic, Ösel. Please get me one-before I die!"

"Yes, Ama-la. The young obey the old. I was going trading soon anyway."

"Oh, thank you, son! But be careful. There might be thieves and swindlers who will try to take advantage of you."

"Why, Ama-la!" Ösel cried scornfully. "What's wrong? Have you no faith in me? I trade so well that I could sell . . . foot-warmers in the hottest hell." His eyes sparkled brightly. "If birds had money, I could sell them used feathers. I could even sell old garbage to – "

"Yes, my son. You've always been a clever one. But please make haste! The pain is getting worse. And India is so far away! Please leave as soon as possible."

"Yes, Ama-la. I'll travel fast. I'm young and strong."

few days later, Ösel set out on the road, perched atop a brown horse. His five mules carried a lumpy load.

Soon he joined a trading caravan. He rode beside a short, fat man with bulging arms and tousled hair.

"Hello, young lad. What have you got on those mules?"

"Old furs," Ösel lazily replied.

"Oh-tse!" The man gaped at Ösel, goggle-eyed. "Furs? For India!? You must be mad. It's hot down there. Old furs, too! You can't trade those."

Ösel shrugged. He turned his head slightly– to hide a sneaky smile. "We'll see," he said.

or many days, the caravan moved steadily. Some of the men sang songs, while others joked and laughed.

At night, beside the fire, a bearded man with gleaming eyes told boastful tales. He paused only to drink from a large jug.

Ösel listened, but said little. No one bothered to wonder what he was plotting and planning in secret.

It was such a long journey! Sometimes the weather was cold and harsh, but the caravan marched bravely onwards.

One day, they crossed the mountain pass. A howling wind blew fine snow, like white sand, against their faces.

Then the trail began to curve slowly down. The sun felt warmer, and the air grew hot and humid. On and on they trudged. The men became impatient, and their throats were parched.

At last they reached the market place. It was so noisy, so colorful! Crowds of people pushed and shoved. Bales and bundles stood everywhere. Some of the traders argued loudly, face to face.

There were so many things to see and do! You could buy sweet things to eat, exotic drinks. There were dancers, jugglers, and a magician with a green parrot who suddenly disappeared and then screeched loudly out of thin air . . .

At one side sat a thin man in a broad-brimmed hat. He had a bright display of necklaces and rings, shining in the sun.

Up to this man Ösel slowly led his tired mules. "Good day!" he called cheerfully. I'll trade you these rare, expensive things for your necklaces."

The man stood up. "What have you got there, lad?"

"Some nice, warm furs. They're very rare."

"Warm furs!? You must be joking! The summer heat has just begun. It's hot enough to fry an egg."

Ösel nodded. "Right now it is, of course," he said. "But have you heard the prophecy?"

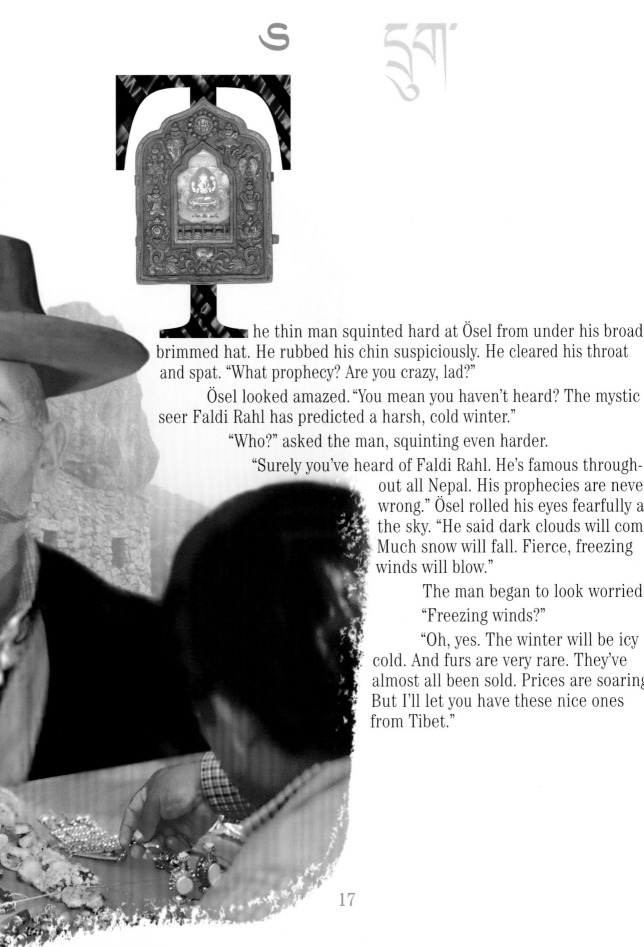

The thin man squinted hard at Ösel from under his broad-brimmed hat. He rubbed his chin suspiciously. He cleared his throat and spat. "What prophecy? Are you crazy, lad?"

Ösel looked amazed. "You mean you haven't heard? The mystic seer Faldi Rahl has predicted a harsh, cold winter."

"Who?" asked the man, squinting even harder.

"Surely you've heard of Faldi Rahl. He's famous through-out all Nepal. His prophecies are never wrong." Ösel rolled his eyes fearfully at the sky. "He said dark clouds will come. Much snow will fall. Fierce, freezing winds will blow."

The man began to look worried.

"Freezing winds?"

"Oh, yes. The winter will be icy cold. And furs are very rare. They've almost all been sold. Prices are soaring! But I'll let you have these nice ones from Tibet."

v

Meanwhile, Ösel's mother sat at home, praying devoutly on a small wool carpet she had made. She prayed for the sick and the poor. She prayed with all her heart for all beings to have less pain, to have less suffering.

Sometimes she dared to picture the sacred relic that Ösel would bring. It was a vague shape that glowed warmly in her mind. But then she thought: "No, I'd better just pray."

One day, all of a sudden, she had a feeling that her son was near. She got up slowly from her carpet . . .

Yes! Ösel was coming down the road on his brown horse! And there were his mules, too. They carried a smaller load now.

She met her son outside the door. He embraced her very tenderly. Then, smiling, he held her by the shoulders. Joy brightened up her wrinkled face.

"Dear Ama-la, you look better now."

"I do feel better, Ösel. I think my praying helped somehow."

He ran to his mules, returning with a small bundle. "Look, Ama-la! Precious necklaces! And I have many, many more!"

"But where . . ." she said meekly, "where is the sacred relic, son?"

Ösel slapped his head. "I forgot. There was so much to do. But you can choose any of these beautiful necklaces you want."

"Oh, Ösel, I need a sacred relic! You must go back. Oh, please, please go!"

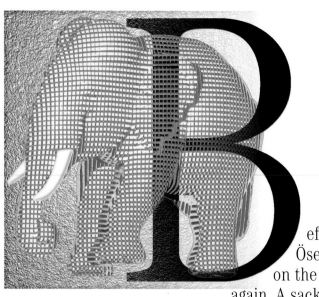

Before long, Ösel set out on the road again. A sack of cheap, shiny ore was tied across the back of each mule. Already he was grinning, for he had devised a bold, new plan.

He joined another caravan. He made the long, hard journey south. The trading post was even busier than before.

This time, Ösel approached a fat man wearing a turban.

"Good day, sir."

"Good day, young friend."

Ösel pointed to his mules. "I've got a load of white gold to sell," he declared. "It's freshly mined, very pure."

"White gold?" said the man. "Never heard of it."

"What did I tell you, sir! It's so rare, many people don't even know it exists. But it's much more valuable than common, ordinary gold." Ösel's eyes grew wide.

"Especially this pure kind. This lot was mined from a rich, new deposit. If you can't appreciate its value, sir, I'm sure someone else will be glad to—"

"Hold on there, lad," the man interrupted. "Of course I've heard of white gold. I just wanted to see if you knew what you were talking about."

Soon Ösel was back on the road, his purse bulging with money. He hummed softly to himself.

But when he reached home, his mother looked much worse. Her face was drawn and withered. She smiled weakly. "Where is the relic, Ösel?"

He gasped. Once again, he slapped his head. "I guess it slipped my mind," he said.

"Oh-tse-la!" she lamented, sinking to her knees. "My son, you've got to get one! Please!" A large tear glistened in her eye. "For if you don't, I'll surely die."

he next morning, Ösel gathered up a lot of old grain sacks. Using a sharp knife, he cut each sack in half, pausing only to laugh at his own cleverness.

"This scheme," he said to himself, "is even better than the white gold trick. And it's even funnier than Faldi Rahl."

He loaded the rough cloth on his five mules and journeyed to India once again. Smirking slyly, he reached the trading post. At one end, a pretty woman was selling fine silks and cotton cloth.

Ösel led his mules up to the woman and bowed respectfully. "Good day," he said. "I wonder if you'd be interested in a special bargain?"

The woman regarded him skeptically. "And just what bargain might that be?"

Ösel took a piece of grain sack from the nearest mule. He held it carefully in both hands, like a precious item of great value.

"The famous Doctor Fizzadred has treated this rough cloth," he said, "with special herbs to heal and beautify the skin. You wear it, and they all sink in."

"Does it get rid of wrinkles?" the woman asked. "Will it make me look younger?"

"Well . . . yes," said Ösel. "As a matter of fact, it does that too. Just rub it on your face three times a day."

The woman leaned forward excitedly. "I'll trade you even," she said. "One piece of fine silk for each cloth."

"Why not?" Ösel's eyes sparkled brightly. "Sometimes, it even works on scars and warts. But, to tell the truth, not always."

"Why, you honest young man!" the woman exclaimed. You can have this cotton too." Soon Ösel's mules were loaded with fine silk and beautiful cotton cloth. Humming happily, he began the long journey home. When he was almost there, he thought: "My mother will be proud of me. I traded so successfully."

But then he stopped and slapped his head. "Oh, curses! Not again!" he said.

sel slumped forward helplessly on his brown horse. "Blast!" he muttered angrily. "It's too late to go back. It would take me too long. She'd die for sure."

Just then, something moved among the scruffy grass and stones beside the road. It was a little greenish-brown toad. It hopped among the scattered skeleton of a dead dog. The midday sun gleamed white upon the picked-clean bones.

Ösel stared intensely into space. A strange expression crossed his face. Jumping from his horse, he bent down to the skull and pried out an old tooth. "If she has died," he grimly thought, "there's nothing I can do. But if she's still alive, this will give her great pleasure."

He wrapped up the old tooth in a square of fancy silk brocade. "What do I care?" he said aloud. "She wants it so much! Is this so wrong? She'll never know."

ༀ ༈ བཙུ་བ་ཚེ་བ་

sel found his mother lying flat on her bed. How weak she looked! She feebly raised her head and tried to smile.

"Ösel! It's you! And I see you brought me something. You remembered!"

"Yes, Ama-la. Here's the relic. I . . . succeeded. Go ahead, take it. Don't be shy."

She held the silk shape tenderly. Her eyes were shining with gratitude. Scarcely daring to breathe, she opened it. "Oh, Ösel! What is this?"

"It's the Buddha's canine tooth, Ama-la."

Her face lit up. She gazed at the tooth in awe. "Oh, thank you, son!"

She said no more. She had already begun to pray. She prayed devotedly for all beings. She placed the tooth on her altar. She made prostrations to it. She prayed simply—but with faith so deep, she saw the relic in her sleep.

She held the tooth reverently in her palm. She circumambulated it. She seemed to gain in strength. It seemed to ease her pain.

A month went by. The tooth was always there— as a support for every prayer. A radiance began to show: her wizened face began to glow.

Ösel watched her sitting on her little carpet, praying with great devotion. "How can this be?" he wondered. "She seems so calm, so peaceful! Has she discovered some great truth? Are there strange powers in that tooth?"

23 བཅུ་གཉིས།

Another month went by. One morning, Ösel came to watch his mother pray. He'd been away, trading. He hadn't seen her for many days.

As he approached the house, piercing shouts rang out. Ösel stared. What were all the neighbors doing there? Why were they pointing upwards?

Ösel gaped in amazement. Above the house, white puffy shapes were floating by, huge puffy clouds in the blue sky. These, he knew, were auspicious shapes. An elephant! A billowy elephant with a long trunk! A great prayer wheel, all snowy white! A stupa, shining with clear light!

And when the last cloud shape had passed, he looked up in the sky, astonished. Like lightning through the empty air shot colored stripes, misty and bright! They arched across the wide, blue sky—a rainbow, dazzling to the eye!

28

Ösel gasped and trembled. "What can it mean?" he wondered. "Did my mother finally reach the state she sought, realization?"

Filled with awe, he rushed into the house and saw: her body was no longer there! Just her clothes, in a rumpled pile, and her hair and nails. One more thing caught his eye. A pearly-white object, like a large grain of rice. It softly gleamed upon the little carpet, where, with such faith, she sat and prayed.

Find out more about Tibet!
Resources, news and links are available
on the World Wide Web at these websites:

http://www.snowlionpub.com
(Snow Lion Publications)

http://www.gn.apc.org/tibetlondon
(The Office of Tibet, UK)

http://www.iem.pw.edu.pl/~jstar/pspt/wtn.html
(World Tibet Network News)

http://www.peacenet.org/ict
(International Campaign for Tibet)

http://www.twics.co.jp/~tsgjp/lthpe.hmtl
(Japan Tibet home page)

Map showing India Tibet
frontier as mutually
agreed upon by the
British and Tibetan
Plenipotentiaries.

[signature]

British Plenipotentiary.

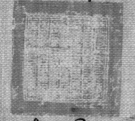

[Tibetan script]

Tibetan Plenipotentiary.

Delhi 24th
March. 1914.